LIST

ALSO BY JOHN THOMPSON

At the Edge of the Chopping There Are No Secrets (1973)

STILT JACK

JOHN THOMPSON

First published in Canada in 1978 by House of Anansi Press Limited. This edition
published in Canada in 2019 and the USA in 2019 by House of Anansi Press Inc.
www.houseofanansi.com

House of Anansi Press is committed to protecting our natural environment.
As part of our efforts, the interior of this book is printed on paper that contains 100%
post-consumer recycled fibres, is acid-free, and is processed chlorine-free.

23 22 21 20 19   1 2 3 4 5

Library and Archives Canada Cataloguing in Publication

Thompson, John, 1938–1976, author
Stilt Jack / John Thompson.

Poems.
Originally published: Toronto: Anansi, 1978.
Issued in print and electronic formats.
ISBN 978-1-4870-0666-2 (softcover).—ISBN 978-1-4870-0671-6 (EPUB).—
ISBN 978-1-4870-0672-3 (Kindle)

I. Title.

PS8589.H488S75 2019   C811'.54   C2018-906092-1
                           C2018-906093-X

Library of Congress Control Number: 2018962467

Series design: Brian Morgan
Cover illustration: Willow Dawson
Typesetting: Sara Loos

 Canada Council   Conseil des Arts    ONTARIO ARTS COUNCIL
for the Arts   du Canada   CONSEIL DES ARTS DE L'ONTARIO

*We acknowledge for their financial support of our publishing program the Canada
Council for the Arts, the Ontario Arts Council, and the Government of Canada.*

Printed and bound in Canada

RECYCLED
Paper made from
recycled material
FSC   FSC® C103567
www.fsc.org

CONTENTS

INTRODUCTION BY ROB WINGER

I've stuffed my laptop into a plastic bag, ascended a marble staircase, and pushed each hand into a disposable cotton glove. It's 2008, ten years ago. Spread out on the table are poems handwritten on mid-1970s paper placemats, on an airline motion sickness bag. A huge, black hardback writing book is jammed with couplets, private inspirations, pronouns without antecedents. I'm at the National Archives in Ottawa, doing research on John Thompson, the poet I've been circling now for a decade. All that's tangibly left after the fire that took his papers, the police that took his rifle, Tobin, and the "blind, stupefied heart" from the opening couplet of *Stilt Jack* are these scraps of paper, I'm thinking. But what gives me the right to see them? Shouldn't what begins in privacy stay private? Is the reading of all poetry, then, a kind of home invasion?

Turning over a ripped piece of paper, this one from a 1974 package of king size Belvederes, I find a possible answer, written in Thompson's distinct script: "the user is / the content of the poems." This statement tells me a lot about the work that *Stilt Jack* does, the worlds it still opens. All of us, I'm thinking, are users — aren't we?

Other boxes on the table yield more privacy. More character. And, inevitably, more caricature. Ever since *Stilt Jack* first appeared in 1978, two years after its author's death, the book has been informed by its own legend. So James Polk, a friend of Thompson's and an editor at Anansi, where Thompson's first book was published in 1974, wasn't wrong when he said (in 1991) that it's possible to read *Stilt Jack*, chillingly, as a "brilliant suicide note." Thompson was thirty-eight when he died, after all; and *Stilt Jack* has exactly thirty-eight poems. So maybe we can't blame those those who, when reading *Stilt Jack*, actively consider the various disintegrations its author experienced during his brief writing life: the collapse of his marriage; the denial of tenure by his university; his crusty disappointment in the supposedly lukewarm reception of his first book; his mental illnesses and alcoholism; his lonely house out in Jolicure, New Brunswick — a gusty landscape filled with tiny, complex creatures that bury into every available crevice — only thinly insulated, without the daughter who'd left with his wife, and missing his late-life lover, who lived at the time in another province. A house that eventually burned to the ground the year before he died. That there's both beauty and pain in all this is easy to see. And we're drawn, I think, to tales of brilliant self-destruction, of difficult genius. I feel that pull here, too: to talk about Thompson's expert mountaineering, about his bringing his rifle to the poetry classes he taught at Mount Allison University, about knives stabbed into pub tables, about privately toasting Thompson's grave with a group of fellow admirers out in Jolicure one fall. But I worry that such voyeuristic admiration ultimately detracts from recognizing what Thompson really achieved in his work.

So, rather than forwarding another *ad hominem* celebration of Thompson's troubled character, I think it's important, here, to stress the intellectual consideration, refined formalism, and deeply allusive history that makes *Stilt Jack* so singular. The measured claim by maritime poet Peter Sanger, the world's pre-eminent Thompson scholar, that *Stilt Jack* might be "the most allusive book in Canadian poetry," after all, is not simple arithmetic. Thompson's allusions are both formally chosen and profoundly personal, intentionally controlled and openly intuitive. Yet, for years now, Thompson has been reduced to a Romantic, rifle-toting, alcoholic, masculine cliché. He's seen first and foremost as a troubled genius, an angling Van Gogh, a postcard fiction. While that might be a vital part of the story, there's a lot more happening here than personality.

Part of *Stilt Jack*'s complexity has to do with other poets in different cultural geographies. But the book's declared form — the ghazal — is not the traditional ghazal of Rumi or Ghalib or Hafez or the practitioner Thompson seems to have admired most deeply, Mir Taqi Mir. As the great American ghazal poet Agha Shahid Ali noted, after all, some counter-cultural English-language poets writing ghazals in the 1960s sometimes didn't seem to know the form's original precepts, rhythms, or rules. Instead, they tended to pick what they liked — an illogical disjuncture between couplets, a simultaneous address to higher and lower powers, a complex focus on grief and loss and love, a shared system of symbols, a direct naming of one's teachers — and to abandon the rest, ignoring the form's fundamental stringencies, metrical strictures, and cultural roots. What was left, a form many of us now call "the free-verse ghazal," is not the same form as the traditional one, whose English-language version, I should add, continues to evolve in a parallel lineage alongside the version Thompson initiated in Canada. Ali referred to those written in the traditional form as "real ghazals in English"; the ones in *Stilt Jack*, for him, I'd bet, were part of a vast complex of appropriations. "For those brought up in Islamic literary traditions, especially the Persian and Urdu ghazal," Ali explains, referring to the explosion of the English-language free-verse ghazal in American poetry since the 1960s, "to have many of these arbitrary near-surrealistic exercises in free verse pass for ghazals was — is — at best amusing."

But, like so much of what's resonant in *Stilt Jack*, Thompson's knowledge of the form was *not* merely naïve or absent-mindedly colonial. A skilled translator, Thompson was researching the form's history as early as 1973, planning to translate fifty of Mir's ghazals into English for a book, the working title for which was *Mir Taqi Mir: Ghazals in Translation*. According to his notes, he'd also planned a thirty-page introduction for the project, which would detail Mir's place in the Urdu ghazal tradition. He wrote to ghazal experts seeking sources, insights, information. He read both "free-verse" and traditional versions. He made careful notes on conventions and customs. His own ghazals, when he eventually wrote them, then, were considered and respectful, not blindly misinformed. In *Stilt Jack,* he seems to have intentionally replaced Mir's Muslim devotion with his own High Anglicanism and the form's original cultural references with the trout populating the Tantramar marshes, a geography he embraced wholeheartedly, circling it on a map, the story goes, when deciding where to accept a professorship in 1966. He personalized and reshaped the form to examine his own relationship with the poets he most admired. As did Aijaz Ahmad (the Urdu linguist whose 1971 transliterations in *Ghazals of Ghalib* did more to establish the free-verse ghazal's conventions than any other volume), Thompson made careful formal choices for *Stilt Jack*, attempting to pay respect to what was traditional without pretending that he shared the ghazal's specific cultural heritage, tenets, or ideals. He adapted rather than adopting, altered rather than annexing. His choices, it seems to me, echo Ahmad's defense of the free-verse form that Ali quite rightly derides when it's engaged without consideration. "The fact is," Ahmad argues,

> formal devices, such as rhymed couplets or closely scan-
> nable prosodic structures are, in contemporary English as
> opposed to the nineteenth-century Urdu, restrictive rather
> than enlarging or intensifying devices. The organic unity
> of the ghazal, as translated into English, does not depend
> on formal rhymes. Inner rhymes, allusions, verbal associa-

tions, wit, and imagistic relations can quite adequately take over the functions performed by the formal end-rhymes in the original Urdu.

I think so, too. But such a categorical declaration, depends, of course, on the skill and self-awareness of any given poet. And it's also absolutely true that few free-verse ghazal poets have ever been as skilled as Thompson was, as willing to research the form's history, as careful. It's also worth noting that Thompson would have read Ahmad's defense; he mentions *Ghazals of Ghalib* in his research notes.

Can traditional forms evolve, then? Should they? Are they always beholden to their original strictures? Are Thompson's careful considerations enough? Does he have any right to adapt a form without the precise insights that cultural membership almost always enables? I see arguments on both sides of such debates — arguments that deserve respect. But I think we should also recognize that no matter what sort of traditional formalism it engages (or alters), *Stilt Jack* is an exceptionally rare sequence, a book none of us can ever really emulate successfully, especially considering its epic, horrifying, beautiful intimacy. As maritime poet Harry Thurston once asked of Thompson's masterwork, after all, "how can you possibly approach what he's pulled off there, or want to?"

Regardless of its formality — a formality often overlooked or overshadowed by Thompson's own histrionics or legendary illnesses — *Stilt Jack* remains one of the most compelling poetic sequences ever published in Canada, a book that, as Lorna Crozier notes, "quickly became a classic among writers, passed by word of mouth and from hand to hand." That's certainly how I first found it. It's only in the last few years, in fact, that Thompson has been anthologized in the Canadian mainstream, discussed as canonical, finally given his due. But the barbs and stars of *Stilt Jack* are still sharp more than forty years after they first appeared. And they remain immediate. *Stilt Jack* continues to set the writing lives of young writers on fire, to launch them into absolutely new understandings of, as Thompson puts it in ghazal XXI, "how small a poem can be: / the point on a fish hook." Whenever this occurs, it seems to me, it feels for each new poet like a personal connection, a private one. If "the user is / the content of the poem," then, might every reading of *Stilt Jack* be a kind of self-portraiture?

Back at the archives a decade ago, I'm holding Thompson's hand-made leather satchel, assembled at the Sackville Harness Shop down the street from where, as an undergraduate, I first discovered poetry and photography, Buddhist philosophy and love, feminism, the salt marsh, the sea. It's the bag that carried his notes, his black writing book. His keys, maybe. What parts of the archive will always remain sealed, I'm wondering? What happens if we open them?

Years later, my doctoral dissertation long finished, my own tentative ghazals collected in their slim volume, I remain unsure. Maybe that lack of definition is part of what's so essential about Thompson's private pain and wonder in *Stilt Jack*. In his hands, the form gets drunk and goes to church, stays home and watches the hockey game, strides out into the marsh and drops its lines into the water. That space and energy matters; it's somehow at the heart of how we read these poems now. Knowing what we know about its composition and publication, its author's personal life and its form's public one, reading *Stilt Jack* has become an exercise in shared privacy and public singularity. In his hands, the ghazal, Thompson writes, "is the poem of contrasts, dreams, astonishing leaps." Such reverie is something all of us could use.

Maybe this is why it feels important to remember that every nightmare-laden valley in *Stilt Jack* is echoed by journeys through summit fever to the very highest peaks. To remember that, no matter how often we read it, *Stilt Jack* always ends with a new heart, one no longer "blind" or "stupefied." As we continue to celebrate this exceptional meditation on what it means to be here, it's worth remembering that *Stilt Jack*'s final lines will always offer each of us a private gift: "Can't believe it, knowing nothing," Thompson writes, right at the end, in the present tense. "Friends: these words for you."

Rob Winger
October 2018

Works Cited

Ahmad, Aijaz, ed. *Ghazals of Ghalib: Versions from the Urdu by Aijaz Ahmad, W.S. Merwin, Adrienne Rich, William Stafford, David Ray, Thomas Fitzsimmons, Mark Strand, and William Hunt.* New York: Columbia University Press, 1971.

Ali, Agha Shahid, ed. *Ravishing DisUnities: Real Ghazals in English.* Middletown, CT: Wesleyan University Press, 2000.

Crozier, Lorna. "Afterword: Dreaming the Ghazal into Being." In *Bones in Their Wings: Ghazals,* 51–74. Regina: Hagios Press, 2003.

Polk, James. Introduction to *I Dream Myself into Being: Collected Poems* by John Thompson. Toronto: Anansi, 1991.

Sanger, Peter. *SeaRun: Notes on John Thompson's Stilt Jack.* Antigonish, NS: Xavier Press, 1986.

Thompson, John. Black Book. *John Thompson Fonds.* National Library and Archives of Canada.

——— . "The ghazal". Research Notes. *John Thompson Fonds.* National Library and Archives of Canada. c. 1973.

——— . "Mir Taqi Mir: Ghazals in Translation." *John Thompson Fonds.* National Library and Archives of Canada.

——— . *Stilt Jack.* Toronto: Anansi, 1978.

Thurston, Harry. "The Iconography of the Maritimes: Interview with Janna Graham." *White Salt Mountain: A Gathering of Poets for John Thompson,* edited by Anita Lahey. *Arc Poetry Magazine,* 62 (Summer 2009): 41–44.

Winger, Rob. *The Chimney Stone: Ghazals*. Gibsons, B.C.:
    Nightwood Editions, 2010.

ROB WINGER is the author of three poetry collections: *Muybridge's Horse*, which was a *Globe and Mail* Best Book, the winner of the CBC Literary Prize, and a finalist for the Governor General's Literary Award, the Ottawa Book Award, and the Trillium Book Award for Poetry; *The Chimney Stone*; and *Old Hat*. Born and raised in Ontario, Rob currently lives in the hills northeast of Toronto, where he teaches at Trent University.

STILT JACK

GHAZALS

Originating in Persia, the ghazal is the most popular of all the classical forms of Urdu poetry. Although the form as it is now written first appeared in Persia, it probably goes back to the ninth century. The great master of the ghazal in Persia was Hafiz (1320–1389). Five hundred years later, Ghalib, writing in Urdu, became an equally brilliant master of the form, which is full of conventions, required images, and predetermined postures.

The ghazal proceeds by couplets which (and here, perhaps is the great interest in the form for Western writers) have no necessary logical, progressive, narrative, thematic (or whatever) connection. The ghazal is immediately distinguishable from the classical, architectural, rhetorically and logically shaped English sonnet.

The link between couplets (five to a poem) is a matter of tone, nuance; the poem has no palpable intention upon us. It breaks, has to be listened to as a song: its order is clandestine.

The ghazal has been practiced in America (divested of formal and conventional obligations) by a number of poets, such as Adrienne Rich. My own interest in the "form" lies in the freedom it allows — the escape, even, from the brief lyric "unity." These are poems of careful construction; but of a construction permitting the greatest controlled imaginative progression.

There is, it seems to me, in the ghazal, something of the essence of poetry: not the relinquishing of the rational, not the abuse of order, not the destruction of form, not the praise of the private hallucination.

The ghazal allows the imagination to move by its own nature: discovering an alien design, illogical and without sense — a chart of the disorderly, against false reason and the tacking together of poor narratives. It is the poem of contrasts, dreams, astonishing leaps. The ghazal has been called "drunken and amatory" and I think it is.

John Thompson

[NOTE]

John Thompson completed *Stilt Jack* shortly before his death in 1976. Apart from the correction of some minor typographical errors, the preface and the poems are presented here as they appear in the original manuscript, without editorial changes.

For my daughter, and for S.

Those great sea-horses bare their teeth and laugh at the dawn.
W. B. YEATS

May God preserve the sickness of my eye.
TRUMBULL STICKNEY

I have only to lift my eyes, to see the Heights of Abraham.

I

Now you have burned your books: you'll go
with nothing but your blind, stupefied heart.

On the hook, big trout lie like stone:
terror, and they fiercely whip their heads, unmoved.

Kitchens, women and fire: can you
do without these, your blood in your mouth?

Rough wool, oil-tanned leather, prime northern goose down,
a hard, hard eye.

Think of your house: as you speak, it falls,
fond, foolish man. And your wife.

They call it the thing of things, essence
of essences: great northern snowy owl; whiteness.

II

In this place we might be happy; blue-
winged teal, blacks, bats, steam

from cows dreaming in frost.
Love, you ask too many questions.

Let's agree: we are whole: the house
rises: we fight; this is love

and old acquaintance.
Let's gather the stars; our fire

will contain us; two,
one.

III

It's late. Tu Fu can't help me. There's no wind.
My blue shirt hangs from the cuffs on the line.

I can't talk to God. Tonight, I dug
three hills of potatoes. Sadness, what's that?

Give up words: a good knife, honed; and a needle
drawn across an iron bar, set in a matchbox.

Damn these men who would do my work for me;
my tomatoes redden by the window.

All spring and summer (this inch,
these noosed three moons) I fished trout.

One line of poetry dogs me; the newspapers,
the crazy world.

I'm thinking of you. Nashe. Rats on my window sill.
The dirt under my fingernails.

Lord, lord. I'm thinking of you.
I'm gone.

IV

I fed my marrow with the juices of clams,
oysters, raw onions, moose heart and black olives:

a green crust, a man banging a raw
elbow-bone on my table, stopped me.

I thought all women were beautiful, and I was ready:
drunk, I'd lie with dark iron; sober, walk away.

There's a health will lead me to the grave, the worm;
resisting axioms, I'll dream,

lie down on my right side, left side, eat dung:
Isaiah greets me; he wants to talk; we'll feed.

V

Don't talk to me of trifles; I feel the dirt in these:
what brightens when the eye falls, goes cold.

I have so many empty beer bottles, I'll be rich:
I don't know what I'd rather be: the Great Bear, or stone.

I feel you rocking in the dark, dreaming also
of branches, birds, fire and green wood.

Sudden rain is sweet and cold. What darkens
those winds we don't understand?

Let's leave the earth to be; I'm asleep.
The slow sky shuts. Heaven goes on without us.

VI

My daydreams defeat me, and cigarettes;
in the cold I'm myself: two follies.

I want to cut myself off. Bone says:
I'll dance, and you with me.

Bats flit at close of eve; anger
dies with the wind; partridge roost.

The moon, the moon, the moon.
A pine box; Herodotus; no tears, a settling:

what lies in its right place, lives. Brothers,
sisters, true friends lie down in darkness.

Dreams and the cold: I'm drunk on these.
Sisters, brothers, fathers, friends, I don't forget.

VII

Terror, disaster, come to me from America.
Middle of the night. Highs in the seventies. Penny Lane. Albany.
                                        Albany?

What letters of van Gogh I remember, I've forgotten.
He cut off his ear. Crows. Potato eaters.

Crazy squash, burnt tomatoes, char of poems, sour milk,
a candle gone down: is this my table?

I'm waiting for Janis Joplin: why,
why is it so dark?

I talk to a poet: he goes on, drunk:
I pray he's writing, don't dare ask.

Hang on, hang on: I'm listening,
I'm listening to myself.

VIII

I forget: why are there broken birds
behind me; words, goddammit, words.

I want to wake up with God's shadow
across me: I'm a poet, not a fool.

Porcupine are slow, fast in their quills:
they'll come to your iron bar, believing themselves and apples.

I don't want to die bloody on the highway:
I travel back roads, the dirt;

don't complain about going: sometimes
think I'll never get to sleep.

Everything reminds me. I want to push.
Black spruce; strange fires.

Snow will come. Wind. A kind of age.
What's at my feet must move quickly.

October; 3 A. M.; I go out and take a rose,
and the sea, and thorns.

I want to give everything to this burnt flower: I've nothing;
I bury my face; set it in water.

IX

Yeats. Yeats. Yeats. Yeats. Yeats. Yeats. Yeats.
Why wouldn't the man shut up?

The word works me like a spike harrow:
by number nine maybe I get the point.

It's all in books, save the best part; God knows
where that is: I found it once, wasn't looking.

I've written all the poems already,
why should I write this one:

I'll read Keats and eye the weather too,
smoke cigarettes, watch Captain Kangaroo.

Big stones, men's hands, the shovel
pitched properly. The wall of walls rises.

If I weren't gone already, I'd lie down right now:
have you ever heard children's voices?

Sometimes I think the stars scrape at my door, wanting in:
I'm watching the hockey game.

Likely there's an answer: I'm waiting,
watching the stones.

X

A pineapple tree has grown in this kitchen
two years, on well water. Right here,

a man went to set a fire in the stove
and the blaze froze on the match.

Those winds: in summer turn the head rancid, in winter
drive a cold nail through the heart down to the hardwood floor.

Daisies, paintbrush, bellflower, mustard, swamp iris;
hackmatack, crowns driven northeast: they're there.

Pigs fattened on boiled potatoes; horses mooning in the hay;
in the woodshed he blew his head off with a shotgun.

XI

The fox is quick; I haven't seen him; he's quick.
The rainbow strikes one foot at my door.

The kettle lid lifts: must be fire,
it keeps.

It's too dry to plough; gulls grow in the cut corn,
owls, harriers: so many swift wings.

There's all the noise here,
it's so quiet:

the sky sleeps on the backs of cattle,
streams slow to black.

Last night I died: a tired flie woke me.
On White Salt Mountain I heard a phrase carving the world.

XII

after Tu Fu

I'm here at last, love this bed:
we stay up at night talking the moon down.

A bad mistake: looking for new flowers,
finding frost.

We'll fish tommy cod: that's enough;
come April I know where to go.

If the man gives me enough pennies
I'll go across the marsh and buy a little field.

Why be my own Job's comforter?
A bottle of cheap rye: an empty head.

XIII

The rook-delighting heaven?
I've seen one crow.

The cock pheasant I'll nail: he's beautiful,
quick; I know the tree, the spot; He's disappeared.

They dragged him home behind the tractor:
fat beef; the dark wound in the loam.

I think we should step out the door:
they're calling: men, women and dead voles.

I wish there were less wine: I'd want more;
breasts, breasts.

I'm in touch with the gods I've invented:
Lord, save me from them.

XIV

All night the moon is a lamp on a post;
things move from hooks to beautiful bodies. Drunk.

I think I hear the sound of my own grief:
I'm wrong: just someone playing a piano; just.

Bread of heaven.
                    In close.

In dark rooms I lose the sun:
what do I find?

Poetry: desire that remains desire. Love?
The poet: a cinder never quite burned out.

XV

If I give everything away
it's because I want to take everything;

catching things from the air, I'll force
a perfect flower from the blue snow;

I can look at the sun with open eyes,
the moon laughs in my kitchen;

I think of children and the unwise:
they have terrible strength;

when will you,
will you?

The drunk and the crazy live for ever,
lovers die:

our mouths are wet with blood:
is it the blood we'll live by?

If I give you my right arm,
will you

XVI

The barn roof bangs a tin wing in the wind;
I'm quite mad: never see the sun;

you like sad, sad songs that tell a story;
how far down on whiskey row am I?

I believe in unspoken words, unseen gods:
where will I prove those?

If I wash my hands will I disappear?
I'll suck oil from Tobin's steel and walnut.

If one more damn fools talks to me about
sweetness and light...

I'm looking for the darkest place;
then, only then, I'll raise my arm;

someone must have really socked it to you:
were the lips made to hold a pen or a kiss?

If there were enough women I wouldn't write poetry;
if there were enough poetry

XVII

I pick things out of the air: why not?
No one shall sleep.

Lift me up, lift me up..., he said:
I would have, I would.

I don't need Page's arm:
I've got fire: I'm laughing, laughing.

We've all been cold. I was born mad.
Wooden matches strike anywhere.

If there's joy for one day, there is, there is:
they that sow in teares: shall reap in joy.

Celebrate. Celebrate. Celebrate.
Death cannot celebrate thee.

One fish, one bird,
one woman, one word,

that does it for me, and the last word of *Ulysses* is
yes.

XVIII

A man dancing into life:
ashes to ashes; O my America.

Friends, I believe I'll burn first:
I'll find you by compass: dead reckoning.

Sing no sad songs. A tree stands:
lay a stone against it.

Cast a cold eye, cast
a cold eye:

when I meet you again I'll be all light,
all dark, all dark.

XIX

I try for oblivion, dirt
and a woman:

my right hand breaks;
new snow;

I drive into a strange heart, and lift
out of all this beauty something

myself, a fish hook tinged with blood,
a turned furrow,

potatoes, fish, those who love them,
must come.

XX

I begin again:
why should not young men be mad?

Trial of my own images, I dream
of one thing.

The curve of a line weaves
a celestial equator:

My child. The dark
horse in the rain.

Let Merton speak, but leave
the numbers lie as stones.

I pick over
last night's food.

Now let us servants rise like Atlantis.
By lying down, I'll wake, depart in peace.

The tide ebbs from my hand.
I want to join blood.

Loaves of bread remembered:
eat salt and tell the truth.

Grief the knife, joy
the vulnerable bread.

Eat, let the blade
be surprised by joy.

XXI

I know how small a poem can be:
the point on a fish hook;

women have one word or too many:
I watch the wind;

I'd like a kestrel's eye and know
how to hang on one thread of sky;

the sun burns up my book:
it must be all lies;

I'd rather be quiet, let the sun
and the animals do their work:

I might watch, might turn my back,
be a done beer can shining stupidly.

Let it be: the honed barb drowsing in iron water
will raise the great fish I'll ride

(dream upon dream, still the sun warms my ink
and the flies buzzing to life in my window)

to that heaven (absurd) sharp fish hook,
small poem, small offering.

XXII

I'm just a man who goes fishing:
if there's a woman with green eyes, there is.

My land's wet: I'll wait, perched on a post;
I know my seeds will alarm the sun.

Dark April, black water, cold wind,
cold blood on a hook.

I won't scream when I die:
I've burned everything;

words swarm on the back of my hand.
I don't run,

thick with honey
and sweet death

I love to watch the trout rising
as I fall, fall.

XXIII

What is it you want to say? Say it now.
I hear children; the fallow; pig's blood.

Churn, churn; all in black:
the milk I want, I want.

There must be an end:
flowers deceive me;

we are all poor, poor:
the cattle lift their huge eyes.

Where am I? Where are you?
The Lord stuck on a bulletin board.

Put two words together: likely
it's your name.

I don't know mine:
the words have taken it, or someone's hand.

I dream myself into being,
a poor man.

I'm a great fish, swallowing everything:
drunk all my own seas.

Say it now: honey from the sweet, drunk, dead:
I lift my eyes,

I'm listening; the moon sinks;
I chart the back of my hand.

I don't hear your words: I hear the wind,
my dreams, disasters, my own strange name.

XXIV

Always the light: a strange moon,
and the green I don't understand;

knives set in order; somewhere else,
eyes looking back across a terrible space:

a meeting in a garden, hands, knees, feet
in the dirt: animals; the flies feeding;

what comes for this? pour wine on it:
have you read all your blood?

No prophecy in the furrow: only the print of bare feet,
anxious for what grows;

nothing? one small leaf is a heart:
a leaf we divide, dividing us.

Lift up the soily stones,
feel the burn of lime,

a handful of seeds, a handful of earth,
silence in thunder on the tongue:

a long waiting without stars,
ending in snow.

XXV

In a dark wood,
and you in a strange bed.

In midsummer I dream great snows
and a man come to ask about fish.

Divinity sounds in machines,
shines darkly from the pleasure of birds.

What do I believe? I hear the crack
of corn fattening at night.

The blood at night sounds
with your swimming.

Where are all our books and stories?
I look into dark water:

we have been there: our eyes
join deep below the surface.

If I ask questions, you'll show me
some beautiful thing you have made.

XXVI

Surrounded by dirty glasses, nights
of love: the world is full of…

and then to be honest, as a hair,
a still hand, a plain box;

caught by bad music, strange meat,
the smell of old tin;

there are ways, and signs: the woods
point one way,

the words: there is a word:
there are words, lie about us,

dogs and the night and children
poured out in looseness

and children
on the grassy ground.

XXVII

You have forgotten your garden (she said)
how can you write poems?

That things go round and again go round.
In the middle of the journey...

Folly:
the wildflowers grow anyway.

I wait for a word, or the moon, or whatever,
an onion, a rhythm.

All the rivers look for me,
find me, find me.

The small stone in my hand weighs years:
it is dark.

To turn, and remember, that
is the fruit.

XXVIII

I learn by going;
there is a garden.

Things I root up from the dirt
I'm in love with.

First things: lost. The milky saucer,
of last things a siren.

Please, please be straight, strait,
stone, arrow, north needle.

I haven't got time for the pain,
name your name,

the white whale, STILT JACK, in her face,
where I have to go.

The Lord giveth.
I wrote letters,

sealing,
stitches of emptiness.

Absence makes what?
Presence, presence.

Music, beautiful stories,
tin, tin cans,

fingers on a pine table,
fire.

Love, black horse, a turned
head, voice:

breaking my heart, laughing;
knife, fork and spoon,

turnips, stored words, rip-rap and all that
etcetera,

something
taken away.

XXX

The mind tethered, head
banged with a hardwood stick;

sense a mangled iron
and the fire gone cold.

Read it all backwards; start with Act III;
a clean pair of heels.

The muck of endings; drunk beginnings;
yattering histories, rodomontades, anabases.

Get to the bloody point:
seize the needle,

day, plainness: cold sea, that
one grain of sand.

XXXI

I'll wait; watch
Look, look.

Poor people. Poor
We're rich; beautiful.

Brant: the Great Missaquash Bog:
My love: a splash: safe.

I fire my right arm out strait.
My wife's sledgehammer; my woman's eye.

I'm not good enough.
Sufficient is Thine arm alone.

XXXII

A woman to quench the fires of my eye:
song: sweet, comely song.

We sing hymns: we care
for the sound of grief and the grieving.

But we'll dance, her ashen hair
tenting my body;

we join hands, eyes, lips: one:
as safe as a toad in God's pocket.

Love the final loss, the last
giving.

This is the day which the Lord hath made;
we will rejoice and be glad in it.

XXXIII

Dark as the grave. The deep lightning
whiteness of swans' wings.

I make necklaces for a woman and
my daughter: gentle harvests.

Anger dies with the wind. In near-sleep
I'm a salt-water trout spilling seed.

The want. The hunting harrier
bound to earth. The fox denned.

I go clothed like a bear: ride
against the sun. Then the snow sleep:

I have only to lift my eyes to see
the Heights of Abraham.

XXXIV

I surrender to poetry, sleep
with the cinders of Apollo.

Belay to words:
Stubai, Kernmantel, Bonnaiti,

Karrimor, K.2., Nanga Parbat,
Jumar, Eiger, Chouinard, Vasque.

Annapurna. The mountain wakens:
a closing hand.

Love lies with snow, passion
in the blue crevasse. Grief on summits.

Let me climb: I don't know to what:
north face, south face?

Maybe the roping down,
the last abseil.

XXXV

after Mir Taqi Mir

Love, look at my wounds, the shame I've drunk –
I wouldn't wish such suffering on my bitterest enemy.

Walk the graveyards: did you know the dead could have such
hair?

But devouring fate would have gnawed at them forever.

You're well off: don't make your home with this history of
disasters:

The cold desert always destroys my bed.

I know: your pale green eyes speak what's final:
Sweet deaths never spoken of, beautiful terrors.

It's clear: the broken moon is suddenly full for me.
As always, drops gather into a limitless ocean.

XXXVI

I don't know

Desire.
Taste of the sea: salt.

The scorch of letters written
from the poem's isolate place.

I feel all the weight:
have I dared the dark centre?

We'll rise as one body.
A wedge of geese.

Time: slow as rivers,
entering us as the wings of birds.

Soft now. The join deep as bone.
Safe as the unwounded sap.

When you look into my eyes,
The moon stills as a Kestrel.

We'll gather all our lives and deaths
In a lightning harvest.

XXXVII

Now you have burned your books, you'll go with nothing.
A heart.

The world is full of the grandeur,
and it is.

Perfection of tables: crooked grains;
and all this talk: this folly of tongues.

Too many stories: yes, and
high talk: the exact curve of the thing.

Sweetness and lies: the hook, grey deadly bait,
a wind and water to kill cedar, idle men, the innocent

not love, and hard eyes
over the cold,

not love (eyes, hands, hands, arm)
given, taken, to the marrow;

(the grand joke: *le mot juste:*
forget it; remember):

Waking is all: readiness:
you are watching;

I'll learn by going:
Sleave-silk flies; the kindly ones.

XXXVIII

Should it be passion or grief?
What do I know?

My friend gives me heat and a crazy mind.
I like those (and him).

Will it all come back to me?
Or just leave.

I swing a silver cross and a bear's tooth
in the wind (other friends, lovers, grieving and passionate).

I've looked long at shingles:
they've told.

I'm still here like the sky
and the stove.

Can't believe it, knowing nothing.
Friends: these words are for you.

JOHN THOMPSON was born in Manchester, England, in 1938. He studied in England and the United States, and taught for nine years in the English Department at Mount Allison University in Sackville, New Brunswick. He lived in the Tantramar Marsh country, an area which provided the imagery for much of his writing. He died in 1976.

A LIST

The A List